# Letters to a
# *Lover*
## I Never Had

MEGAN PARKER QUINN

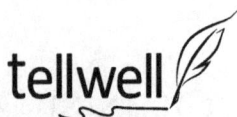

tellwell

Tellwell Talent
www.tellwell.ca

ISBN
978-0-2288-0363-8 (Paperback)
978-0-2288-0364-5 (eBook)

music has a way of putting melody
to the feelings that are in one's heart


do you love to listen to
music while reading?
Here is a Spotify playlist
that is curated just for this book
http://bit.ly/letterstoaloverIneverhad

to lissa

my constant reminder
that life is too short
to not do brave things

Prologue & true story:
a white moth landed on my right hand
the day I started again . . . again
a sign from Spirit to follow the light

Dream:
you sent me a white moth
it held the same frequency as you
I found it on a staircase
it settled on my fingers
as though it were always meant to be there
drawn in by my light

your name was brought up
the moment I said out loud
that I decided to leave another

for the record
you were not my idea

I was supposed to be alone
with heartbreak & shame

I thought that I was not worthy
of finding another

always in fear of being alone
constantly pushing people away

it would be me
distracting with work

it would be me & my littles
forever trying to make a home

you weren't supposed to happen

before I even met you
even without me
you were perfect

— mpq

I had forgotten that
we had met before on a day
where both of our friends needed us

I can't remember your face
or who you were
or what I said

all I can remember
is that your shirt was red

"those two should be together"

someone said
someone who doesn't say things out loud
unless it's really, REALLY important
someone who has yet to be wrong

the more you came up
in conversation
the more I started
to realize that you
were important

there was healing
that needed to be done first

things left behind
before I could be
brave enough
to meet you
again

but remember it this time

I had asked the Universe a long time ago
to be friends first with my future partner

that is what I have been given
an incredible chance to be

your friend first

that is what I shall be
if you allow it

thank you
for accepting the friend request
that I sent at 3:30 in the morning
that important day
from Las Vegas


I was sober
(honest)

When I found out
that you were also a
    reader of books
my knees gave out
        as I swooned
    just a little
while waiting in line

for airport french fries

mpq

one of our friends' children
called out your name
one day while we were
outside on an adventure
& you were walking into your house
(I'm the girl next door)

that was the day
I discovered a skill I didn't know I had

being able to snatch words
out of the air
words that I don't want people to hear

you were wearing a red shirt

I don't know how it started
or what it was about
it didn't really matter

but it didn't take long
for your messages
to be my favourite

my intention was to be brave
& see you again face-to-face

over & over I asked

over & over you chickened out
manifesting a reason to say no

that was the start
of the little yellow bird

I started to think
I had made it all up

that our paths crossing was being missed
by moments for a reason

why would fate tease me
with someone so perfect

so soon after burning down
yet another life

with someone
who was anything but?

even if it wasn't going to turn
into anything at all
you were denying yourself
the opportunity to have a friend

until I called you on your shit
then you showed up
first for yourself
& then at the door

wearing grey this time

I don't think
we looked
each other in the eye
at all that first time
we went outside together

I do remember
that first hug
you gave me
& the way my heart wall
recognized yours

I remember it meant nothing & everything

I remember talking about everything & nothing

I remember the sun & how fast we walked

I remember not being able to breathe

I remember being lost but not lost at all

I remember it not feeling like the hours that it was

I didn't realize what it was at the time
only that I remembered what it felt like

as I picked a yellowing leaf
from a moulting tree
as I explained who it was that I am
& what it was that I do
& that it's not my job to change anyone's mind

that I felt your energy reach into mine

the blisters from the walk
were as big as the feelings
I had for you
& just as fucking painful.

mpq

that first day is when
I discovered your currency
of mountains & water


specifically, hot water

you have stronger hugs
but my energy is undeniable
so much so
that people seek it out

you can't control everything
you say to me


well . . .
I can TRY

Dream:

we sat across from each other
you, weaving stories of what
has been happening in life
me, trying to flirt
pushing my foot on your leg
you put your hand on my foot
we exchanged energy that way

(which sounds weird when I write it out
but wasn't at the time)

that weekend
as I taught others magic
was the first time that I saw
& had validated
(a LOT)
what the future could be with you

also, that I needed to start
growing out my hair

go with the flow, you said

be the boat
be the boat
be the boat

I repeated over & over my mantra

all weekend
every card
every reading
all my own advice being dealt back to me
all the fucking boats

it made me seasick

before I even knew what was happening
my heart would start
to pound in a way
I didn't fully understand yet

it would stop me from working
it was all I could do
to sit in the energy
& try to breathe

this is when I started to wonder
if this was how it felt
when you were
thinking of me

I hugged you around the waist
feeling both of our surprise
about how well we fit

it was the one time
I was able to lay my head against your chest
& hear your heartbeat

over & over & over again
the future kept coming up with you in it

it started as a hopeful vision
but now it seems like a curse

the hope that was in my heart
was shattered as you made a statement
a post that dug you deeper into a hole
I knew you didn't want to be in
a hole you knew
you didn't want to be in

the hardest part about it all
has been watching
my friend
not follow their heart

we are all lost

you choose to be on a path
that is hard on you
thinking that the pain that you feel
will undo mistakes that were not all yours
that somehow you deserve it

who am I to remind you
that that's not true

If I were to pick you
up in the morning
& drop you off 12
hours later & tell
you to bring runners,
a bathing suit & towel

would you be brave
enough to come on an
adventure with me?

you know that scene in *Aladdin*
where he is standing on a flying carpet
asking Jasmin "do you trust me?"

she doesn't know why, but she looks at him
with skepticism in her eyes
knowing that her heart is saying yes

that part?

you're Jasmin

a moral dilemma
was solved
with clear boundaries

something you hadn't
had before with a friend
who just happened to be a girl

I have a confession

I wrote a cheque for you
let me explain — it is how I make my magic

pay to the order of myself
for a one-day trip in the mountains with you
signed from the Universe

created September 21
(the 21 always being a day for magic)
dated for September 25

*cashed on September 26

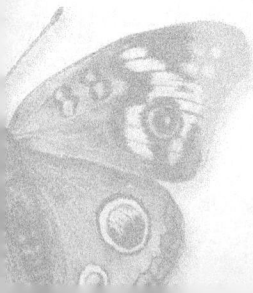

it's funny
how honest a person can be
when trapped inside a car
with another
who is also magical

I didn't need to look at the map
my heart always knew
where it had to go

I can hear my heart better
when I am with you

it is incredibly delightful
to know that there are other people
on this planet who get that same feeling as I do
when finally arriving in the mountains

it is hard to describe
because it is different than
*home* or *safe*
but it's along those lines

it is a word that has you breathe deeper
that has you look up & around
that quiets your mind
an energetic pull to the Earth

the word might be grounding but with you
it's stronger than that
perhaps a word that isn't English
maybe it is meant to be a feeling & not a word at all

we kept finding
all these magical spots
full of fairies
that neither you nor I
admitted to seeing

It happened that day

A significantly insignificant moment

When I saw how you see
The light like I do.

You are a light seeker

This is the moment where I first
started to not stop myself
from falling in love
               with you


mpq

the mountain on one side of us
the water on the other
a fallen tree my alter
I stopped

shaking, I unwrapped my magic tricks
feeling them & my guides sigh in relief
this was what they had been intended for
this moment

you trusted me to cleanse your energy
you trusted me to connect you to the Earth
you trusted enough to allow yourself
to listen to your heart
to breathe

when I put my palms on yours
an older part of you remembered
you saw something that day
a secret

I saw something that day too
that you also have the incredible gift as a lightworker
that one day — together — we could help so many
& how beautiful you are

that hug was different
than all the others before
than all the hugs since

hugging back, I whispered
"you are remembering"

you turned the tables
using my tools to do the same for me

I closed my eyes
following the feeling of your heart

I didn't understand
how you knew what you were doing

you felt different
I don't close my eyes around others

when I opened my eyes again
after you put my hands in prayer
in front of my heart
something strange happened


you weren't afraid to look
at me anymore

my first gift
a string with a spell
one of intention

to remind you
that it doesn't have to be
so hard all the time

to remind you
perhaps
a little of me

in all my life
I don't remember
anyone offering their hand out to help me up

in all my life
I don't remember
not wanting to let go

not having a reason to hold on
in that moment
it was my turn to be Jasmin

you asked me a question
that no one had ever asked me before
it might be the most important question
I had ever been asked
I almost didn't believe it when I heard it
to which I answered my favourite

willow

the water always has such wisdom
it has carved pathways out of the mountain

even though it has fallen
it moves strongly still

not caring which path it takes
only that it needs to get somewhere important

I lie by the river to feel its power
asking for it to help cleanse me of my grief

the mountain still beneath me
cold but there — supportive & strong

the sky above blue
open to infinite possibilities

as you lay beside me to experience the same
you never make me feel like I am crazy

you adventure the same way that I do
you picked the same path
you stopped where I wanted to stop
you stole moments like me

I could feel our paths starting to align
there was so much of me that wanted to stop it
a growing feeling of doubt
that I wasn't healed enough

by the time we reached the bridge on the way back
I understood the healing I needed to do
was for me
to be with you

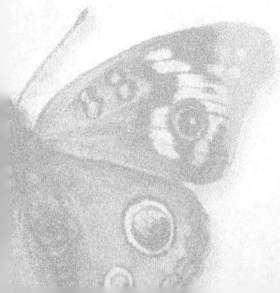

We both breathe better
when we are in
the water

mpq

it snowed
on a sunny day
while in healing waters

the sky
the mountains
the forest

they were all happy
that we were together
there for that one day

you were breathing
    relaxed
    funny
    unguarded
    yourself
as I drove you home to be in the arms of another

before I fall
asleep
every night
I say
thank you
for everything
that I am
grateful for

that night
I was
grateful
for that
one day
with you
knowing that
it could be
the only one
I ever get
& that
that
had to
be enough

lots of friends
appies
drinks
lots of drinks
cards
maple whisky
you always sitting beside me
(I missed that part)
a game
a dance where I said that this was awkward
I didn't understand what was really happening
until I felt the way you asked
"is it?"

I didn't know

contacts out
glasses on
sobering up

I didn't know

a show from the neighbours
dishes
you were stalling

I didn't know

we were face to face
with your hands
on my back

then I knew

I asked what you were thinking
to which you denied anything
(you fucking liar)

then you asked what I was thinking
& because I can tell my truth
I raised up on my tiptoes to show you

you were wearing a red shirt

it wasn't sparks or butterflies
it was something different

it was good different
but still different

I don't think either of us
realized what it was

be cool
be cool
be cool
downplay it
don't be weird
be cool
it's cool
it was no big deal
it doesn't change anything
it changed everything
don't make anything out of it
don't fuck it up
be cool
be cool
be cool


"hey"

skydiving?
yes
scuba diving?
yes
bobsledding?
yes
hang gliding?
yes
parasailing?
yes
rock climbing?
yes
ice climbing?
yes
stay in a tree house?
yes
hotel underwater?
yes
hot springs anywhere on the planet?
yes


I will always say yes to an adventure
just. like. you.

going to hang out
at someone's house
for the first time
is like visiting an animal in a zoo

awkward because
you see them
in a habitat that is theirs
but it is not their home

them asking you to judge them for it
hoping you understand that this
isn't totally them
it's not where they truly live


I hate zoos

I tried hard to stay calm
to not make it weird
it's only weird if you make it weird

which is exactly what I did
by trying too hard to not be myself
I regret it all the time

that kiss was different

your guard was down
enough to let me feel
how much you wanted me too

that's the kiss I remember

texting back & forth
        all surface shit
more research
that was needed
to gather more & more evidence
to a feeling we didn't know
if we wanted or not

neither of us slept
that night your string fell off

that was when the magic
started to lose its way

mpg

the same trip to the mountains
this time with the ones that raised you

you trusted me enough
to spend that time with your parents

again
it was different

good different
& I think it freaked us both out

do you know
what's a good cure
for being uptight?

a snowball

your mother is a kindred spirit
& told me her darkest secrets

your father is sick
& told me stories from a time before

they breathe better in the water too

it was a very ordinary moment
tying our shoes across from each other

your mother watched me looking at you
your mother watched you looking at me

because when you did
your smile was real & reached your eyes

that's when I realized how much I had fallen
in the forest that day on the mountain

it made me want to run away
from the heart break that was inevitable

mpq

"I know more than you think"

a line followed by confessions
that clicked into place
pieces of a puzzle
that I didn't know
I was trying to put
together

I can't wait to hear
one day
about what
you saw
that moment
we had together
on the mountain

a whisky all together
after a hard day

you had come with a purpose
one you thought you could avoid

you let me feel your heart that day
an attempt to scare me away

leaving, your hug felt different
it felt like goodbye & it was

So, this is the friendzone

super

mpg

it is really no different
than it was
before

connect

silence

connect

silence

connect

silence

connect

silence

I didn't want anything different
than what already was
or anything more

that's not true
I wanted
less silence

I needed to do something
that scared me
but called to my heart

you were the only one
that I trusted
to help me through it

you agreed to go
on a day that is magical
every month for me

I shouldn't trust you
but I know I don't have to explain myself
for you to understand

you helped me to be brave
& conquer a wall of fear
while I was suffering on seven levels on the inside

you reminded me
to not give up
that I had the power to do it all

that was more important than you know
I didn't know how to say thank you
for reminding me I wasn't going to die

so, I said nothing at all

I didn't say what I wanted to that day
I was afraid of pushing too hard
losing you completely

I am at war between
honouring the boundary
of your honesty and my heart's truth

the Universe intervened
as it knows things
that we do not

the water got you there
the water made me brave
looking up into the night sky

to tell you that you felt like home
that I had waited my whole life for you
& you told me your truth in return

that you weren't ready
I wasn't trying to change your mind
I only need to have the courage to speak

I have done many brave things
that might have been the hardest only
because it didn't turn out the way I wanted it to

it was the only time
I have ever said no
to a hug from you


it was taking
everyoning I had
to hold myself together


I was a paperdoll
stitched together with string
& dropped in water


any pressure or touch
I would have fallen apart
completly

— rupg

I am the only one
you ever say no to

or leave forgotten
& waiting

Who am I to be mad at
you for honouring the
time that you want
for your own heart?

nyp

I try to be in flow & not control
I am practicing trusting the timing


it is against everything I was before

a casual visit with friends
permission to put my hands
on your shoulder
to help with your pain
the burden that you carry
for your family
you let me feel your frequency at full strength

it was a frequency
that I recognized
as I had felt it before

that's when I realized
how often your energy checks in on mine
which makes me think
that "not ready"
is a lie you tell yourself
because you are just
as afraid of us as I am

the friendzone
grows to a wider
more vast area
    of silence
    of no response
    or left on read
the endless game
of second-guessing

my brain asked
"why would you want to be with someone who
obviously doesn't want anything to do with you?"

my heart cried
broken
victim again

weeks later
I see it for what it was
you thinking you can push me away


it almost worked

the friend zone feels like
screaming in a room full of people
deaf to your sound

your scream is silent
except to one person
who chooses not to hear it

because you are magic
& I am magic
I can feel when you reach out

my heart starts to beat faster
my breathing syncs with yours
shallow & quick

is stops everything
my Soul trying to escape my body
to come & find you

one day
when we are in the same room again
bravely I will let you feel

magic that is stronger than anyone else
how much my heart
answers the call of yours

I have learned to
love myself
more in perceived
rejection
than I ever would
have found with
you.

mp q

over & over again
I try to move on
but I have fallen
& cannot be persuaded
to get back up

as much as my friends
are tired of hearing about you
& answering my questions
I'm quite sure there is a bet among them
about who is the more stubborn one

I'm going to bet on myself

the death of one of my dearest friends
shifted my timeline of life
it gave me the gift
of realizing what is important
it still hasn't shifted enough
to give me the courage
to show up at your door
naked under a trench coat
like everyone is saying
& very much supported
by my friend
on the other side
who also suggests
to be licking a vanilla ice cream cone
with sprinkles

I never realize
how much I've missed you
until I see you again

I think you feel the same way
an invitation always feeling like a game

with space comes a louder voice
as I ask why all the tests
to which you have no real answer

even though I ask
to not dream of you
I always do

dreams so vivid
I cannot determine
if they are real or not

I was once again brave & asked
if your magic is to be in dreams with me
I'm still waiting an answer

your magic wakes me up
in the middle of the night
when you think you can sneak in
to my Soul
while I am sleeping

you cannot hide your energy from me
like you do with everyone else

I feel myself being
slowly freer of you

I'm able to see things in
a different light & angle

I see so much
of my part in all of it

the space fills with other things
but never any people

that spot in my heart is still
being held by you

my time is not
being wasted
as I wait for you

you have taught me
more about myself
then you'll ever know

even though I'm sure you do
because you know
more than I think

what I don't understand is
what the fuck are you waiting
to be ready for?

what do you feel like first thing in the morning?
what do you feel like after a long time away at work?
what do you feel like when you use your magic?
what do you feel like in the shower?
what do you feel like in the middle of the night?

1:11

accidently your energy reached me
you, too tired to block it any more

sadness, grief & regret washed over me
stronger than it had ever been with you before

still, you chose to
live a hard life

still, I chose to
play the broken hearted

always the offer to listen
always turning me down
forever in the game we play


I should have called you

on one of the hardest days of my life
I saw you for a moment
to bring you a gift
that I had held onto for too long

when it mattered
you were there
to give me back the words
that I often say to you

you are not alone

which makes me angry
because I AM alone
because YOU have chosen
for me to be

as I hugged you good night

my lips said
    Merry Christmas

my heart said
    I love you

my brain said
    Goodbye

I realized two weeks later
that you heard them all

fuck it

you scare me in a way
that I can't run away from
it feels as though
my whole life
has been designed
for us to live
our best lives together

even if nothing more
were to happen
after one date
I am willing to risk
waiting for
that chance

you
are
worth
waiting
for

statistically speaking
there is no fucking way
that so many magical people
could be wrong
with what they saw

it is not your potential
it is not our potential

it is not you if you change
or are different

I don't want to fix you
believe me, I've checked

I only want you to show up
when you say you are going to

when I know that you want to
so that I may see my friend again

I want you to be more you
I want me to be more me

but together

mpg

"even after all of this,
how much of you
    still loves him"


"enough that I have
    not lost faith"


mpg

on the days
where I feel
my faith fading
when I feel myself
wanting to throw you to the wind

I ask for
a sign
a baby bird
a reminder from the Universe
for me to keep
along this path
to help remind me
that I am
not crazy

it has shown up
when you couldn't
as a gif
a book
a shirt
a snowball maker
a giant inflatable
a sign for hot tubs

the Universe was especially proud of that one

Dream:

you hugged me in a way that said
"I miss you"

which were words
I was able to hug back with
as I felt the same
but can never say it out loud
as I never see you anymore

Dream:

you showed up in a red shirt
sweaty
you had run all that way
to come & save me

you pushed my tormentor aside
straddled me as I lay on the floor
dying
drowning in my own air

you held me tight saying
that you were here
in your arms
my hands holding onto your shoulders

I died
feeling safe
for the first time
maybe ever

Dream:

we walked & talked
snow falling in the night sky
these giant Hot Wheels cars all around us
I grabbed your hand to stop from falling
you didn't let go this time
neither of us did

I woke up
still feeling the warmth
of your hand holding mine

in every dream I have of you
you always leave when I am working
making me question

are you afraid of not keeping up?
or afraid of not being strong enough for it?
or afraid of being an example of the teaching?

or is it my fear of being too much for you?
of once again leaving someone I love behind?
or are you afraid
because this is the work you want to do too?

I have waited my
whole life for you –

What is a little
bit longer?

mpq

Dream:

sandcastles
sunshine
laughter
little
little
little
glances of love
gratitude
ocean waves
causing trouble
exploding hearts

Dream:

an island
you — aligned
me — fated
the shade of snow
mermaid hair

Dream:

what if you were my best friend
& lover from a past life?
what if you were the one who betrayed me?

what if the birthmark that I have
in the shape of a heart is from you?
the stab wound that I died of decades ago?

you believed me
kissing the heart that marks my skin to apologize
sealing the contract from that lifetime

Dream:

in the middle of the night
you come home to me
slipping under the covers
kissing me good night
I kiss you hello
thankful you are home
safe again after another journey
grateful that once again
all of our favourite hearts
are under the same roof

knowing the potential
of the future

is a great lesson in

patience.

mpa

part of me wonders how we can be together
or with anyone
when we are still legally tied to others

one day
I won't hear
"I know more than you think"

because you'll feel
safe enough
to actually fucking tell me

I think you hide her from me
your little
who carries the name of my unborn
now the name of a character
waiting to be birthed
she is as magical as you
as magical as my littles
as magical as me

are you afraid of me falling in love with her?
your little who was once mine in a past life?

or are you more afraid of breaking
both of our hearts?

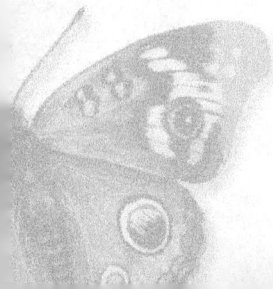

I'm overdue for an adventure, u?
I'm going to the mountains, come with me?
how is your heart?
do you have plans Saturday?
I miss spending time with you
I am forgetting what your laugh sounds like
if you could change one thing about your
life right now, what would it be?
I miss you — a lot

*erases all of it*


"hey"

"your hugs are different"

fucking right they are
they're fucking better
that's with clothes ON

if I had to choose my favourite
between the hugs hello
& the hugs goodbye
I would choose the latter

those are the hugs that have the most feeling

I can't wait to watch Disney movies with you
I have it on my bucket list to sing a duet
with my lover

your pick

what if you were to be
all that you could be

what if I were to be
all that I could be

first by ourselves
then together

we could share our light
starting with our littles

after that
the world

watching you speak about food
the way you remember it
how you describe it
how it always comes with a story
makes me fall in love with you
even more as I can feel
your joy & gratitude
for the smallest of things in life

just for today
any time with you
is enough.

mpq

still
months later
the Universe brings me gifts of you
in the baby birds
in an inspirational quote
in an adventure
a character with your name
(who also struggles admitting with
their love for another)


it's impressive, really

can we spend
the night
lying in
the mossy forest
together
looking at
the stars
enjoying being
together
in silence
in that moment
even if it is
only in my dreams
will you meet me there?


this is the only way
I see you now

you have broken my heart
          a hundred times
I will let you break it
          a thousand more

A broken heart is an
          honour
it means that I have let
     as much love in

As I have let out.

_mpq_

when we start again
IF we start again

no
WHEN we start again

can we start small
so that we both feel safe?

holding hands feels like
a good place to start

then can we promise each other
no more running?

My heart is a
harbour,
& I am waiting
for my boat
& my sailor
To come home
Safely to anchor

*mpq*

there is a song that plays
that reminds me of you

I don't know why
I never heard the song when I was with you
the lyrics don't resonate with our story

I think the Universe is giving me a sign
that one day will make sense

even when I ask the Universe for help
to not be tortured
there is not a night
where I do not
    dream about you
where I do not
    wake up thinking about you

is it not a thing of comfort
to know that we can
check on each other's hearts
while in our dreams?

I trust you enough
to know that you've asked
for space for a reason

I need to learn to trust myself
enough to use
that space for a reason

how can I trust you
to ever show up for me
if you can't show up for yourself?

maybe that
is what you are waiting
to be ready for

you say that you have never lied to me
you've never told me the whole truth either

what if you don't answer back
because you want to keep that true?

how does one wrap their mind
around being with someone who can
      read all your thoughts
      all your emotions
      see your future
      know that you are lying
      (even if you think you're telling the truth)
      call you on your shit
      hold space for you
      respect your boundaries
      truly see you for who you are
      want you to be the best that you can be
      know what the Universe is trying to
      get you to do & be in life?
it scares so many
including me
but courage isn't about
not being afraid
courage is about
knowing that the potential
of an outcome
& what is true in your heart
is more important
than standing still

you & I
are no strangers
to doing hard things

it is impossible
to untie my heart
from you

I have tried
so have others
it cannot be done

the pain
is too much sometimes
I want to be rid of it

I don't know why
you don't want it untied
which is why it cannot be undone

I will wait for you in the middle
where the knot is
in self-inflicted pain until you meet me there

when I think about all I want in life
where my life is headed
    what to do
    where to go
    what to build & create
part of me wonders how a whole other person
that comes with a little person
will fit into that

then another part of me
doesn't doubt it at all
because as I was designed for you
you were designed for me
our littles chose us
knowing what they were getting into
we are used to making our own rules

I want to love being by myself
as you are also learning

I want to strive for greatness
as you also have ambition

I want to explore the world
you & me & the littles

I want to be seen
to see you

I want us to be alone
together

I have never
second-guessed myself
as much as I have with you

I am no longer available for self-doubt
I know what the fuck I want

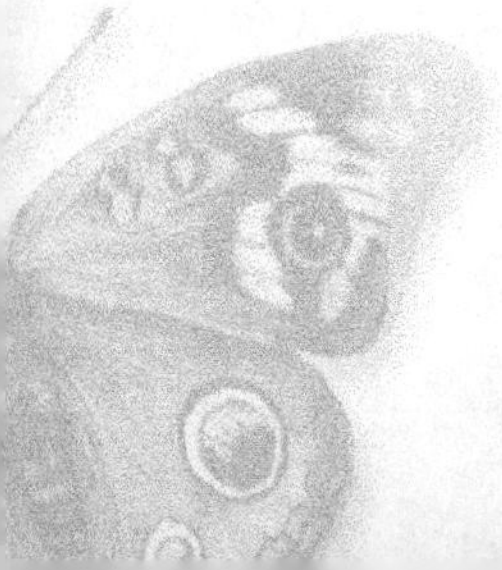

every so often
I think of looking somewhere else
in the beehive

then remember
that I am the Queen here
there is no searching

you will find me
when you are ready
*adjusts crown*

I will not put my life on hold for you
I will continue to live my life as I intended
waiting for the day
that you are ready to join me
& the dream life I have curated

I am afraid
to completely let you go
risk never seeing you again

you are a weight
that I can no longer
choose to carry

it is holding me
back from the life
I want to live

We trusted each other on the mountain
little by little
that trust was broken down
taken away
until only the memory was left

it is now faith

there is something to be said
about the journey of heartbreak

    it fucking sucks

even though
it is necessary to grow again

I've decided
to no longer
think about
what you're waiting for
from me

I'm going to own
who the fuck I am
trusting that it will
not only inspire others
but maybe even for you
to do the same

the Yang is masculine
filled with
    light
    ambition
    action
has amazing deltoids

the Yin is feminine
filled with
    darkness
    restoration
    power
has eyes that twinkle

you are my light
as I am your dark
together we are balanced
in harmony

I am no longer available
to not be exactly who I am
      with all of my power
      with all of my darkness
      with all of my light
I will live my life
leading with love
instead of chasing it

I am completely surrounded by friends
to practice letting love in with

there will be a day when I no longer tie
all my worth into being loved by you

that is the day where I will remember
that I am my own boat

unintentionally
for the last four years
I have surrounded myself with hearts
that are my soul family

I no longer fear being alone
I am anything but

thank you for reminding me of that
on that day so close to Christmas
when I felt nothing but loneliness
even when I was with you

I do not want
to be distracted by others
fucking with the timeline

I said I would wait
wait I shall

some days
more patiently
than others

it is hard to not remind you how
life was easier
when I was in it

I miss your hugs

I miss the feel of the pull on our hearts

I miss your stories & the way you tell them

I miss seeing how you smile

I miss you avoiding looking at me

I miss your name showing up on my phone

I miss you being there for me

I miss being there for you

I miss talking about everything & nothing

I miss our magic

I find myself forgetting about you
when I don't want to

I don't know how to hold onto
something that isn't even there

but that's exactly the point
isn't it?

I dream of you using your magic
doing what you have chosen to do in this life
I see how much good you do
I see how many people you help
I see how simple
           easy
           fun
life is for you

a full heart
I see the joy in your true purpose
you are powerful

I watch you do other things in the meantime
I feel you talk yourself out of your greatness
allowing yourself to think that you are not worthy

regardless of whatever is happening
between you & me
I still see the good of your heart
I believe in you
I will continually remind you of it
until you believe it yourself
& start making some better fucking choices

you have been
are
will always be
worth
every ounce
of energy
I spend on you

I draw from
an infinite resource
one day
I will teach you
to do the same

I will let you break my heart
a thousand times more
this is what I was made for

I am stronger than you
& shall endure it

it is the warrior within me

I try not to be that girl that imagines forever
that can't stop thinking about you
the rest of our lives together
but it is who I am
I love hard & always
I want the small, stolen moments
now & when we are old
not the big grand gestures


just. like. you.

I promised myself
I wouldn't apologize for
who I am any longer
or what it is I want

I'm not going to apologize
for wanting the rest
of my life with you
there is so much I still don't know about you

you are a soul mate to my heart
this is not our first lifetime together

how long will I have to wait
to not have to let go
when we say goodbye?

I will wait until you find another
even then, I think I would still wait
I don't think I could help it
knowing it is yet another distraction
from your true path

I will wait until you
actually show up
when you say you're going to

you are no longer perfect

I can't help but love you just the same

or perhaps, even a little bit more.

nupq

I can't wait to argue with you
about stupid shit

it is your laugh
that I cry about
not being able
to remember

Dream:

In your arms
your hands in my back pockets
watching you realize
how much you're in love with me
before a kiss to end all kisses
waiting in line
to have our books signed
by our favourite poet
Mine worn, an old friend
Yours new, full of hope

mpg

it's not often that I don't get what I want
I will not be distracted

I will learn my lesson in patience
as you learn yours

it is new & unsettling
to feel safe with another
as you realize
you haven't ever had that before

I am not afraid of your darkness or your demons
you cannot overpower or scare me
I will not judge you
you cannot push me away

I designed & chose this life
I have been practicing
for this moment
for us to be together

I worry
    think
    wonder
how your heart is doing

I can't help it
caring about you
is a part of who I am now

is love ever truly wasted?


it must go somewhere

when I'm with you
it is as though I am the wilderness

the river & the waterfalls
are the energy within me

the trees are steady & only whisper in the wind
they are quiet like my thoughts

then my heart feels like the mountain itself
grounded & pulled to centre from the inside

never wavering on who or what it is
not worrying about the season

it is just there
you in me

I am not allowed to worry about you
to ask questions or have answers
I cannot say I miss you

it is not my right

this is when I realize
I'm even farther outside
the friend zone now

my mouth can't even open more
to silently scream
you are too far away to not hear me

one day
I will have the chance
at being your best friend
to adventure with
but like, forever
in life


(it doesn't sound this creepy in my head)

we've each had a few mistakes
lessons of the heart

there has been much heartache
loss followed by an empty void

that we are working on filling
ourselves & not with others

we're learning from our mistakes
that is what makes what we could be
mean so much more

we know how much it means
how much hard work it takes
neither of us wants to fuck it up . . . again

the depths of the feelings
I have for you are unexplainable

it is like trying to describe
to my children how big
the Universe really is & that it's always expanding
& how tiny we are in it

do you worry about bringing our families together?
about where we will live?
about how it will all work
with the other parents of our children?
about how I feel about your work?
about how you feel about mine?
every time I start to worry about these questions
I see this movie scene play in my head
it is of you kissing me
your hands on my face
my hands on yours
bringing our foreheads together
us saying to each other
that we will figure it out
like we have
a thousand times before

this time & all the times after this
we'll figure it out together

grief that comes with death
I have learned
cannot be rid of

we only learn how to carry
how much our hearts
miss the ones we cannot hug
or how we cannot tell them
        how much we miss them
        how much they might have hurt us
        how much we loved them
some days filled with tears

grief that comes with heartbreak
I keep learning
is the same

loneliness
is the price I willingly pay
for stating
that I am no longer available
to be distracted
while I wait for a day
that may
or may not
ever come to be

my brain wants to yell & scream
that I wish we had never met
that I wish I wouldn't have asked you questions
that you weren't so easy to talk to
that you didn't ask any questions back
I wish sometimes
that nothing had ever happened between us
that I didn't know the things that I know
maybe then it wouldn't be so painful
my heart cannot ignore
the undeniable connection
gravitational pull we have
that is what I chose to hold onto
even when it could be the death of me

every time

every time I try to talk myself out of it
of doing the thing that Spirit inspires me to do
I try so hard to fight it
to fight you
how I feel
I can't fight with the Universe
Spirit is too loud
& I have asked for help
I have to be okay to play the part
of the girl who is lovesick
for the boy that wants none of it
I will take that judgment
know the truth
until my heart is directed somewhere else
or I stop being guided to leave presents
on your doorstep

I carry with me grief —
    my love for a friend
    that feels trapped
    inside my body with nowhere to go

I carry with me courage —
    the truth of my heart
    the conviction to follow it
    even when others don't understand

I carry with me doubt —
    trying to keep me safe
    keeping the heart we worked so hard at
    putting back together again protected

I have learned to speak to all of them

one day
neither of us
will be afraid
to look
each other
in the eye

one day
one of us
won't have
to look
away first
because
we feel
too much

why do they call it lovesick?

it is not something that can be resolved
with fluids & a few days of rest

it should be called a love infection
or disease

for one there is a cure
a hope that soon the worst will be over

the other you need to learn to live with
because now it is a part of who you are

it is not your job to protect that piece of my heart
you yourself said that you were not ready
to carry the weight of

I am sorry that I keep forgetting
that I keep giving you a piece in times of need.
then always coming back to you for them

that isnt being fair to you at all

mpg

I cannot fall out of love
with you.

mpg

one day
I hope that you'll
stop
saying no to
me & you

one day
I hope that you'll
start
saying no to
everyone else

& start saying yes
to your own damn heart

what if I were to stop playing the victim in this story?

what if I were to stop wishing you were the hero?

what if I really did just go with the flow?

be the boat again?

what's the worst that could happen?

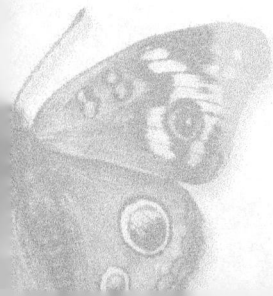

I release the expectation
of an immediate result.

I am safe to trust the timing
of the Universe

mpq

I release you

I release you from me
me from you

I will carry the memories
fond treasures in my heart

I release the expectation
I release the hope

I will trust in the timing
I am not meant to understand
I have faith in what will be will be

I release you because I love you
I release you because I love me

thank you

thank you

thank you

mpq

for every book purchased
a donation is made
for a tree to be planted
with onetreeplanet.org
as a tree has given its life for the story
the story will give back life for a tree
in the cycle of abundance


thank you to
my littles
our little-big family
my soul family of kindred spirits
journals & inky pens
the Universe & the signs along the way
my inspiration

meganparkerquinn.com
Insta @meganparkerquinn
FB at Megan Parker Quinn

kindredscc.ca
Insta @kindredselfcarecommunity
FB @ Kindred Self Care Community

CPSIA information can be obtained
at www.ICGtesting.com
Printed in the USA
LVHW110700140920
665941LV00001B/83